ELEGY FOR THE LAST MALE NORTHERN WHITE RHINO

ALSO BY DEAN YOUNG

Design in X
Beloved Infidel
Strike Anywhere
First Course in Turbulence
Skid
Ready-Made Bouquet
elegy on toy piano
embryoyo
Primitive Mentor
7 Poets, 4 Days, 1 Book
The Foggist (a chapbook)
The Art of Recklessness (prose)
Fall Higher
Bender: New and Selected Poems
Shock by Shock

ELEGY FOR THE LAST MALE NORTHERN WHITE RHINO

A Chapbook

Dean Young

Hollyridge Press
Venice, California

Hollyridge Press
P.O. Box 2872
Venice, California 90294
www.hollyridgepress.com

Cover and Book Design by Rio Smyth
Cover Image detail from "White Rhinoceros Battle 8"
by ©Jollyphoto | Dreamstime.com
Author photo by Laura Saurborn
Manufactured in the United States of America by Lightning Source

ISBN-13: 978-0-9843100-9-8
ISBN-10: 0-9843100-9-6

Some of these poems have appeared in:
The Threepenny Review

25 24 23 22 21 20 19 18   10 9 8 7 6 5 4 3 2 1

Contents

What We're Getting Ourselves Into   3

The Romantics   4

In a Carrion Age   5

My Collage Life   6

Faith   8

Title Elegy   9

Flowers As Far As I Know   11

Wake Up Coil   12

What I Learned from Tomaz   13

Die, English Department, Die   14

Dear Decoration Committee   15

Downton Abby Star Trek   16

No, It's Not All Politics   17

The Comforts of No One Listening   18

Appoggiatura   19

Unknown Ode   20

Smaller World   22

Life-Saving Class   23

More Tales from the Crypt   24

I Know You Are Out There & I Want To Help   25

Ideogram   26

My Qualifications   27

Time-Line   28

How to Be a Drunkard on $5 a Day   29

All My Angles Are Many-Footed   31

Fade Out   32

Elegy for the Last Male Northern White Rhino

WHAT WE'RE GETTING OURSELVES INTO

David moves his mouse closer to the rocket.
Sky throws up on the stone lions.
Nick turns the score upside-down
and plays it that way, rubato,
smaller pieces rising into the fire
to vanish like metaphors. No
better time than now to read Lorca.
One idea is a door can be opened
by pressing your forehead against
a sheet of paper. I brought my own
black wire and opiates. Another
is to plant a giant, elemental,
too-bitter-to-eat fruit-bearing
question in your mind and stare
at the sea until the sea becomes
your mind which will feel hyper
hygienic. Go ahead, spend years
in a steel cage counting syllables,
every evening trying to pick the lock
with a duck feather but it's not
a competition. I know a guy who
knew a guy who had some sort of castle connection
but it's silly to expect glaciers
to share. For me, it's the backyard,
maybe a graveyard or sitting in an old
broken rowboat in a meadow until
the silvery spear of Apollo pierces
the left ear producing offbeat ectoplasmic
squawks it's my job to translate.
Of course it hurts.

THE ROMANTICS

After psychology was invented in Germany,
a leaf had a hard time falling without
something tragic happening in childhood.
Every raindrop had the face of a werewolf.
Dream of an ox with a paintbrush,
get yourself to hospital.
Eventually the sky couldn't unetherize
but people kept hurting themselves
with garters, outbreaks of spirit animals,
a greenish sheen available by bottle
and brocades so thick you need
a special needle. Perfect conditions
for the issue of a monster 150 years later
critics still argue is based on Byron,
slavery, galvanization, artic exploration
or miscarriage but one thing's for sure,
you'd better have warm clothing and know
how to suture when you walk into the human brain.
Also a lawyer. A good red. Your current
insurance info and medications,
something for pain, something for rain,
something for the lions.

IN A CARRION AGE

It's only after decades of service
I have come to teach with a burning twig.
Tried a pine cone but today's cohort
can't find it's power source and swears
someone somewhere perhaps not yet born
is being discriminated against so there's no
stopping them from working on their paper
fists for their hash tag parade. Never-
theless, it is my job to profess otherwise
but nothing about ripping your own heart out
or keeping the epiphyses unclosed,
no putting acid in the office party punch
or taking a javelin into the bouncy house.
Clearly they're prerequisites.

MY COLLAGE LIFE

So after being chopped apart,
sown back together from mostly
the same stuff, some 70s prog rock
still sticking out, a few Kafka slips,
how's it feel to be alive?
Like a bee in a bubble bath.
A cigarette in a French movie.
That single golden scrawl
in one of Paul's black paintings.
A piece of sky upside-down
possible from a different puzzle entirely.
Like that turtle we stopped traffic for.
Sometimes a cloud intervenes.
Periods of asterisk.
No one knows what they are either.
Like simultaneously being part
of something huge and very very small.
Tristamagesis in an azurite crown.
Two carbon atoms per cubic meter of outer space.
A glove that tugs itself off
always ends up inside out.
Like digging a trench, filling it with blood,
waiting consultation.
First out of the horse and hacking.
Like a winged presence in the wings
beckoning stage left.
The heft of cathedral tunes.
Exit pursued.
Cog in a crocodile.
Codicil in an organelle.
Another coil in the outer shell.
Like squeezing a lemon lets you know
just how cut up your hands are.
When Mozart in the afterlife
heard about the atomic bomb,

he needed to be alone a long time
with his giraffes. Like through
the hole in my chest comes the conveyance.
Like being turned into an origami swan.
Being in complete agreement with the moon
and anything that survives exclusively
on nectar. Laughter too, just not yet
close enough to tell about what.

FAITH

Putting that toy triceratops
on Emily Dickenson's grave
was not a waste. Giving Jim
that preying mantis chrysalis.
Have you too stood in the susurrus
of the copy room trying to remove
that backwards mask? I don't know
how people can stand it, a party
with so many clowns, a party
with so few. Have you felt
the crackle in the wool? If the rose
inside you also wraps your throat,
now you're talking. Walking into
the birth-of-Venus mist over the frozen lake
was not a mistake. Something was lifted.
Installed. The crocodile is marshmallow
to the ant. To shelter the luminous
ephemerides is not a mistake.
An arrow shot without target
is not necessarily unaimed
but I'd have chosen a conveyance less direct,
more slant, more mossy basket knocking against
unsuicidal waters, maybe a little Sun Ra
at the other end, a glimpse of mother
then the crystal which is where
people say beauty comes from
or its cracks.

TITLE ELEGY

Poor Breton, still trying to install
a burning murmur in our minds
which causes of course problems
at security like what don't? Fruit
is explosive. So's any kind of fluid,
especially tears, especially amniotic,
especially salamanders. In previous centuries,
all you had to worry about was
the filthy flowers, god and an onion crop
then there was a flash
and half the army men melted.
You could see through yourself
to the exploded helix of a mouse,
a few nudes disported,
the construct was crushed
but it kept singing
if you want to call that singing.
Please do.
If only for the illusion
of surviving your own inklings.
Aren't we sick of all the objections
to talking dogs, the tilted arch,
to the statue's genitalia?
The tradition of my feet
ain't no one-way march.
Take anything back far enough,
it's enslaved to a business
we're all cousins to but
I always appreciate the ruse
of being set free
as if the hooks aren't already threaded,
as if the bell's not already drowned.
Lucky for me I love drowned sounds,
I love the skeletal horse sniffing
my ear of another tradition,

the Euripidian scream, the green hand
coming from the cloud's brow and
swan-drawn chariots into the wilds.
Sometimes the usual splatters
can take on an avian manner,
aiding the delusions. What
convincing shrapnel! What
caterwauling from the monkey house.
To stab yourself is redundant.
To board an airplane is redundant.
The world's divided between
those screaming it's going to end,
those screaming hurry
and those screaming who knows what
in the bombed parking lot
but in the gone one I'm from,
a kaleidoscope is the a most
efficacious diagnostic instrument.
What's wrong with me's the same
as what's wrong with a lamb
in a stained-glass window,
the propensity to shatter
imparting a spiritual dimension
just as the moon gives birth to howls,
the heart to a thousand blizzards
and fawns come out at dusk
to eat the white roses left on graves.

FLOWERS AS FAR AS I KNOW

are often associated with mental states
as well as mental institutions but alas,
the language of flowers is much out of favor
among people who think a cultured life
is acting as if you've never wanted to kiss
anything but money. Shakespeare
killed people with flowers. Milton
put flowers in Satan's mouth
but nowadays mention a chrysanthemum
and no one knows what you're talking about:
the sky or your mother,
a nerve in the neck or water allocation?
Sure, a rose can mean love and fecundity
on one side of the mountain,
get the fuck away from me on the other
just like Artemis, goddess of fertility
and ripping men apart so when learning
your medium, ignore flowers at your peril.
When given a lupine by a one-eyed monkey
in dream, let it be your mind clinging
to a California cliff sideways as
a champagne bubble. Not only were flowers
there when and where we were born
but also how and why.

WAKE UP COIL

What I want to say to you can't be said
without delirium just as some moths
can't be touched, only chased as anyone
who's ever been tied to a pole knows,
anyone who's been tugged by a rope.
Blue donkey on the other end. Black hole.
Sometimes when someone's flipped and shook,
nothing but an argument for derangement
spurts out like Byzantium bursting
from an owl's skull. Lots of ants.
Lots of noise from the machine shop
where something we didn't even think exists
is getting fixed. A huge golden window
is hoisted from the sea. Unmummified ibex.
No one gets to hold a snowflake long
without absorbing its fingerprint
but once you've been defibrillated by dawn,
you'll probably shock everyone.

WHAT I LEARNED FROM TOMAZ

Always whisper
when pulling the arms off monsters.
Pizza with a knife and fork.
Wine with dragon.
Blood with song.
What I learned from cunnilingus
is how to stop talking.
If you're lucky, when night falls
it falls through you like a cleaver
so half is free to wander the shimmer
with a metal detector while the remainder
has to work twice as hard to disappear.
It's good to glimpse a mad white horse
galloping towards me with one eye
while the committee simpers on.
Good to be half scarecrow, half flames.
It makes me walk a little strange,
not so much lunge as sudden electron
relocation which may read as stagger.
One of my colleague's saying I've a drinking
problem but she has a desiccated flake
problem. What I learned from chopping
celery is how hard the soul hangs on.
I'm not sure god exists but I bet
sometimes he wishes he did.

DIE, ENGLISH DEPARTMENT, DIE

Sometimes it's a great solace
that everything, palm tree and tank,
paramecium and me, is a vibrating
atomic cloud which is a shell
of probabilities which is mostly
nothing so if I vibrate enough
I should be able to pass through
the toxic dump of this job
like a flame through a flue.
I should be completely free of hydraulics
and blood pressure medications
and not be so threatened by a pile
of lint with the apocalyptic singing
of their births long extinguished in their hearts.
I'm a fish in the sky!
A rubber ball bouncing through walls.
Almost nothing at all.
A blue chip.
That sort of swamp gas
that makes these bleps think
they're under attack from outer space.

DEAR DECORATION COMMITTEE

Friends, it's difficult to talk about poetry
which is why we're all talking at once
about something else: who can use who's
mythology and bathroom, magic mushrooms,
phlogiston, Czechoslovakian milk production,
a single use of the word black in Ovid.
Shining discs have been spotted syphoning
off libraries dot by dot. Did we pump
blood back into the construct just
to club ourselves to death with hood ornaments?
News from the crystal world isn't good.
News from the elephant's worse.
But what's pirouetting in the fire
might not only be ash.
One of us brings a fang.
In rushing water, another sees the face of his father.
One lights his cave with chrysanthemums.

DOWNTON ABBY STAR TREK

Mary texted me at 4 a.m.
Shaef building some sort of fire.
At first I thought the news
I was being warned about was my sick cat.
Something's on my face
so Angie switches the music
out of toothless crooning to a century
more suitable to my tumbril
and flying boots. At least 100
new drawings on the walls of cartoon
beasts struggling with themselves
and their erasures. By what manner
doth the soul pop its piping?
Here's a possum in a dunce cap
attacking a banana. Here's an infringement
on copyright and a tiara'ed bluish smear.
At home my robot launches another rocket
from its chest as tribute to the long lost
alien dinosaur wars, the membrane's
munificence much stretched. Just because
something no longer exists doesn't mean
it's not dropping seeds into your vodka
right now. Sooner or later everyone
coughs up flowers.

NO, IT'S NOT ALL POLITICS

Actually, it's all pterodactyl wings.
To make a perfect swan, fold a splash.
It's about APT converted to ADP releasing
the energy stored in the diphosphate bond
then ink spirals down the arm and dance
twists through the mantis of the leg
and if that don't break the social contract, what?
Most of our genes are invasive species after all.
It's more like taking dictation from a time bomb.
What's it like when you're alive?
Do golden talons clutch your downy breast?
Is everyone else wrong?
Can you drink all the vodka, eat all the seed cakes
and still drive? Is it like lying in warm straw
or blood-soaked? Ballet's about who has the most
holes in the heart for loft. The samba however
married the rigid positioning of the tango with
the suave slouch of salsa we should all be so lucky.
Take a newspaper. Take a pair of scissors.
To be or not to be, what's the diff?
Who hasn't been bit by puppet-shadow?
A rose? Something under the bed? Nowadays
they can snatch stuff from inside us
Hieronymus Bosch could only dream about
and then only if he slept on a toy pyramid.
Might it all be about the girl in 3rd grade
you gave your alien to? Once I saw my own face
in the potatoes but I sure didn't let it ruin
anyone else's meal. We're all locked inside
the same teardrop in the end.

THE COMFORTS OF NO ONE LISTENING

The day may come when you too look up
from your interior notebook in which
nothing you've written makes sense
to conclude, ditto everything.
A sigh comes off the signified.
Food arrives—complete nonsense.
A knock at the door's a knock
on a walnut. By sunset, some ants
have removed the head of an owl
and you can shout We're all going to die!
without referring to the asteroid.
The ephemeral fears you.
The political pees itself.
The best way to sharpen an ax
is to sleep with it. There's a
kind of dancing that's solely staring
into a river, a kind of singing
Keats said was sweetest even though
he was dying of frustration because
it can't be heard.

APPOGGIATURA

This morning I intercepted a verse
of the moon's drafts and urgent song
and knew I shouldn't go to work
with such a tune stuck through my plexus
because I work among corpses
who hate any mention of a personal
heavenly body connection
especially one charged with lycanthropic and tidal surge.
Haven't they ever been charged
by a dark horse in a darker meadow?
When it was time to pick an instrument,
didn't at least one pick a shadow?
The answer of course is always No
but look how excited taxes make them,
wars, the unborn and monetized tar.
Not one of them wants to get caught
grinning like a face floating off in a river
or talk about the wormwood boat of Ra
or the 67th position
where a man brushes a woman with an orchid
and a woman drizzles sugar on a man
or how a struck tree
can store lightning inside itself
until it's finally had enough
and bursts.

UNKNOWN ODE

Historically, the unknown was used
to staunch battlefield wounds.
Now there's a spray. The unknown
assumes too much, says Annabell
trying to break up with herself,
like anyone's even here in the first place.
There are rules about touching
someone else's unknown no one's
learning in grade school anymore.
Here's one now.
Boiling point unknown,
cleave disposition, event horizon,
its animal origami unknown
so stop poking.
I thought the idea was not
to have our brains sucked out
by a giant radioactive leech
or an English department
or is that just me? After
the third surgery, I don't scare
so easily but who isn't jumpy
as an astronaut recollecting
crash landing spontaneously
in the Sea of Tranquility,
O2 running out?
Centuries ago, a little girl
could watch a funny bird
until the hand of god came out
and she became Emily Dickenson
and the universe milkweed
as the quantum predicts.
A lot harder now.
It's all paved over.
God's institutionalized, murderous.
Most of the cosmos won't show up

and it messes with you
so you invent fish blowing tubas,
yo-yoing angels to flesh things out.
Layer after layer of shellac.
Screws in pianos.
Fingerprints in snowflakes.
First you have to love death
says Eluard like it's not
his black raincoat saying it,
like anything his raincoat says
isn't stolen from the rain which
everyone knows around here
never touches the ground.

SMALLER WORLD

Gulls eat the eyes first.
Quartz, compressed,
gives off a shock. Yes,
you should have been warned.
We all should.
About sleeping with sunflowers.
How a wave at its intensest
collapses on itself.
Quick and feathered as a fox.
Perpetual guile of a fugitive grace.
David Bowie is dead.

LIFE-SAVING CLASS

Poetry exists to argue with the wind.
It never wins but the particles
of a person are molded by volition
so how can it hurt anymore than falling
with a lit birthday cake
or having your heart cut out to blend in
even though you're still the same bat skeleton you always were
just a bit more periwinkle-inveigled.
You and your rescue dog.
You and your sandwich punch card,
collection of 18th century surgical instruments,
the 8 millions reasons not to
hardly a feather on the scale.
The tornado makes the mayor come out
in a housecoat holding a house cat.
People are complimented for not
eating each other. Apparently the bloody
footprints stop at the dock where
they're lifting huge sheets of rubber into the air
as if god could be repaired
when everyone knows all you need do
is hold a leaf in your palm
until your hand swings open
until your hand's on fire
then some piano lessons.

MORE TALES FROM THE CRYPT

Despite its supposed jeweled movement
and rocket mechanics, my new heart's
no more accurate, bowstring
still snapped, kitten just as frazzled.
They wouldn't let me keep my old heart
because it was sliced out and burnt
so I wasn't able to take a bite
like any warrior would of his enemy's
to become a greater warrior. Nope.
Apparently not even worth dissecting
or feeding to that emaciated lion
rescued from a Dallas junkyard,
never to be jarred in my office
between my alien skull and complete
works of Vesalius and Robert Fripp
to show where poetry comes from
like when Matthew smashed through
a plate glass door and just kept walking.

I KNOW YOU ARE OUT THERE
& I WANT TO HELP

If you can't describe a rabbit
without dragging in a satellite,
you're still doing better then
those at the top of the class
who can't look out a window
without seeing a dead grandmother,
who's hearts can't beat without
mob-concurrence, taxidermists,
doorknobs, bus drivers, frauds,
little squeaky tenured ducks.
Cartoon music rises from
their microwaved gluten-free ramekins.
The Queen of Counting's dancing
with a picture of herself so
now might be your chance.
Assumes no one washes. Avoid
that old guy who says he's checking
wicks in confined spaces. What starts
as infinitesimal separation
can flower into a full-fledged rip
stirring as the notional anthem
played on a single glockenspiel
sinking into the sea or the statue
of student loan sinking into the sea
or the idea of the sea sinking into
the idea of itself if you want to get
philosophical. Don't. Your earning
power's suffered enough. All that matters
is your promise in the cloak room
after admitting all that previous
experience with burning snowmen
and into your hand was placed
a tiny Mycenaean horse.

IDEOGRAM

A man with a grenade for a brain.
An Aegean.
Sunflower strapped to chest.
Alien vs King Kong vs the Academy of American Poets.
A man his own mouth swallows.
Under-sutured under-study.
Moon on a bicycle.
TV on legs.
The sort of song the rain improves.
Trilobite skull.
Lightning on crutches.
Holy water in the humidifier.
Bullet lodged in Rimbaud's wrist.
Wounded rectangle.
No one.
Nooooo oooone home.
Cyclopic artery open.
It's hard to hold a forest fire overhead.
Same mountain just an inch higher.
Same nova, different bottle.
The mind is sky.
To hear a bell is to wake inside a bell.
To sleep is to be rendered on the celestial rack.
Perfume factory.
Clock in an aquarium.
Heard bird inside the unheard
or the other way around.
Just one big messed-up dot.
Drunk painter with a gull nailed to the wall.
Fixed throb, I'm the guy
who always brings an hallucination
to the knife fight
but I'm not going any further
without my dog.

MY QUALIFICATIONS

I once saw a cloud in a crown
from my hospital room mirror.
Have seen the dead walk, seen them
in fact take over the program.
In any number of cars gone
into corn fields. Sure would like
to get hammered on the blood of Christ.
Would like a bonus. Radiant is the wolf-
faced nightlight of my bedroom. Radiant
the chamomile tea of my convalescence.
Not just once have lasers split my sternum.
Wild and severe, I was chased through the volts.
Pinfeathers grow from the mind
and crickets, I have swallowed.
Yes, it was a mistake to burn
the forest gates, to execute the dragon.
Snakes wriggling from neck wounds,
only then do the grunts make sense
like the old fathers getting up before
dawn to work in the picture tube factory.
That's me sounding like a scream on a laugh-track.
All manner of blue and busted
pottery I have found socketing the ground
with daffodils and tulips and popcorn hyacinth.
Spring comes out of the mouth.
A human heart I've held in my hand,
sadly not my own or Shelley's
or anyone's I've had a conversation with.
Once a stranger at a bar insisted
he owed me 50 bucks but I stopped
the predicament at 20. Once was handed
a bottle of champagne in a line of cars
backed-up by a smash-up in a tunnel.
Then was kissed. Hard.

TIME-LINE

First gladiolas.
Gladiolas with synaptic urge.
Bigger and bigger chirps.
Then squid. Wet gloves.
A bank statement origami'ed into a dove.
Ignoring the protocol at the cyclotron.
Rust dissolving into something warm.
A grasshopper in a bell.
Helping an injured limb out of the road.
Fragility central to the process.
Like no one knows where this bolt's fallen from.
Like putting something in a bag too small
and ending on a preposition.
Like, why not, the head has a balcony.
The lightning-struck minerals sing.
Like jumping into petals.
Darkness soft and without rind.
Light that hurts a lot less
once you realize which parts
of yourself are burning,
which for show.
Suffering is just a ticket stub,
pain just glitter in the mind.
Then, eventually, raptors.

HOW TO BE A DRUNKARD ON $5 A DAY

Who doesn't prefer a shining mind
to another nightshift at the morgue
our mothers tried to warn us about
without any further mention of our fathers?
A shining mind isn't picky about pronouns,
you can mean me, me can mean anything.
A shining mind is less numbing
to the extremities which keep dropping
everything anyway or dropping from,
depending on your mythology.
Whether a yellow jacket flies
into a Coke can like a phone call
beginning the world or god just
wanks off in some waves or
a metal chair's scrapped across the stage
and the mic's live
or the mic's inside a block of ice
in a room with a crucified tree hanging upside down
or a puncture's made
or periplum
or a philosopher runs screaming into the street
to embrace a diseased horse,
the rhyme seeping in
or a couple carbon atoms
bumping into each other in the primordial
get randy
or a big cloud-orphaned hand sculpts some silt
and maybe some diatoms get smashed in
or an astrolabe
such are the voices in our heads
but once you've listened to an ostrich
or put your ear against a walnut
and used a snowflake as a wristwatch
and forgotten your locker combo,

a wine that tastes like aluminum and dust
can still make most bioluminous
the mind's blue sails.

ALL MY ANGLES ARE MANY-FOOTED

Palm trees used to freak me out
until I discovered how many rats
live in them. Had a pet one once
who turned into a pet tumor.
Then my first funeral.
There was the body bourn
on silver foil.
Herb d'provence embalming spices.
The reading of words, spilling of Diet Dew
and the lighting of the eternal flame
which quickly got out of hand
so someone had to get the hose.

FADE OUT

The flashlight my sister swept
across the heavens got no response
either. When my brother leaves his lab,
he's still limping and our governor's demanding
funerals for aborted fetuses and where's
a fetus gonna get the dough for that?
So yes, there are dark shapes in doorways.
Can't be helped. Today, I found a chunk
of amethyst with a face inside you could tell
was willing to wait another million years
for its scream to come out so let that
be a lesson. Ditto the same cuckoo
that followed Tomaz from China
tries to follow me but gets slapped back
for trying to grope the moon and don't I
just don't. Maybe Jay's right that it all
comes down to one untranslatable
fragment of Parmenides. Like when
a dead child is covered with petals
or a goat receives a garland of bells.
It's a thin red thread that holds
the body to the soul. Visibility
is a disguise.

www.ingramcontent.com/pod-product-compliance
Lightning Source LLC
LaVergne TN
LVHW041210080426
835508LV00008B/886